A Mr. Vladimir Stassoff.

Schéhérazade

d'après "Mille et une nuits."

Suite symphonique

pour Orchestre

par

N. Rimsky-Korsakow.

Op. 35.

Partition	Pr. net	M 24 / R 12
Parties d'orchestre	Pr. net	M 36 / R 18
Viol. I, II, Vla., Vcelle., Basse	à net	M 2.40 / R 1.20
Réduction pour piano à 4 m. par l'auteur		M 12 / R 6

Propriété de l'Editeur pour tous Pays.

M. P. Belaieff, Leipzig.

178 – 180.

Scheherazade

Op. 35

Symphonic Suite for Orchestra

Nikolay Rimsky-Korsakov

DOVER PUBLICATIONS, INC.
Mineola, New York

SCHEHERAZADE

Symphonic Suite for Orchestra
based on *The Thousand and One Nights*

Composed 1888. Premiered 1889, St. Petersburg.

PROGRAM

The Sultan Shahryar, convinced of the perfidy and faithlessness of women, vows to marry and execute a new wife each day until no more candidates can be found. But the Sultana Scheherazade saves her own life by interesting him in the tales she tells through a thousand-and-one nights, leaving each story incomplete until the following evening. Impelled by curiosity, the Sultan continually puts off her execution, and at last entirely abandons his cruel plan.

Many marvels did Scheherazade relate to him, citing the verses of poets and the words of songs, weaving tale into tale and story into story.

1

I. The Sea and Sindbad's Ship

40

II. The Narrative of the Prince Kalandar

95

III. The Young Prince and the Young Princess

133

IV. The Festival in Baghdad. The Sea. Conclusion.

INSTRUMENTATION

2 Piccolos [Flauto piccolo, Fl. picc.]
  Fl. 2 doubles Picc. 2
2 Flutes [Flauti, Fl.]
2 Oboes [Oboi, Ob.]
English Horn [Corno inglese, C. ing.]
2 Clarinets in A, B♭ ("B") [Clarinetti, Clar., Cl.]
2 Bassoons [Fagotti, Fag.]

4 Horns in F [Corni, Cor.]
2 Trumpets in A, B♭ ("B") [Trombe]
3 Trombones [Tromboni, Tromb.]
Tuba

Timpani [Timpani, Timp.]

Percussion
    Triangle [Triang(olo), Tr.]
    Cymbals [Piatti]
    Tambourine [Tamburino, Tbrino]
    Snare Drum [Tamburo, Tamb.]
    Small (Snare) Drum [Tamburo piccolo]
    Cassa [Bass Drum]
    Tamtam

Harp* [Arpa]

Violins I, II [Violini, Viol., v.]
Violas [Viole]
Cellos [Violoncelli, V.Celli, v-celli, Vc., V.C.]
Basses [Contrabassi, C.Bassi, C.B., Cb.]

*Harp tunings in this score use traditional German terminology:

Ces	= C-flat	Ges	= G-flat
Cis	= C-sharp	Gis	= G-sharp
Dis	= D-sharp	As	= A-flat
Eis	= E-sharp	B	= B-flat
Es	= E-flat	H	= B-natural
Fis	= F-sharp	*etc., etc.*	

Scheherazade

Op. 35

I.

39

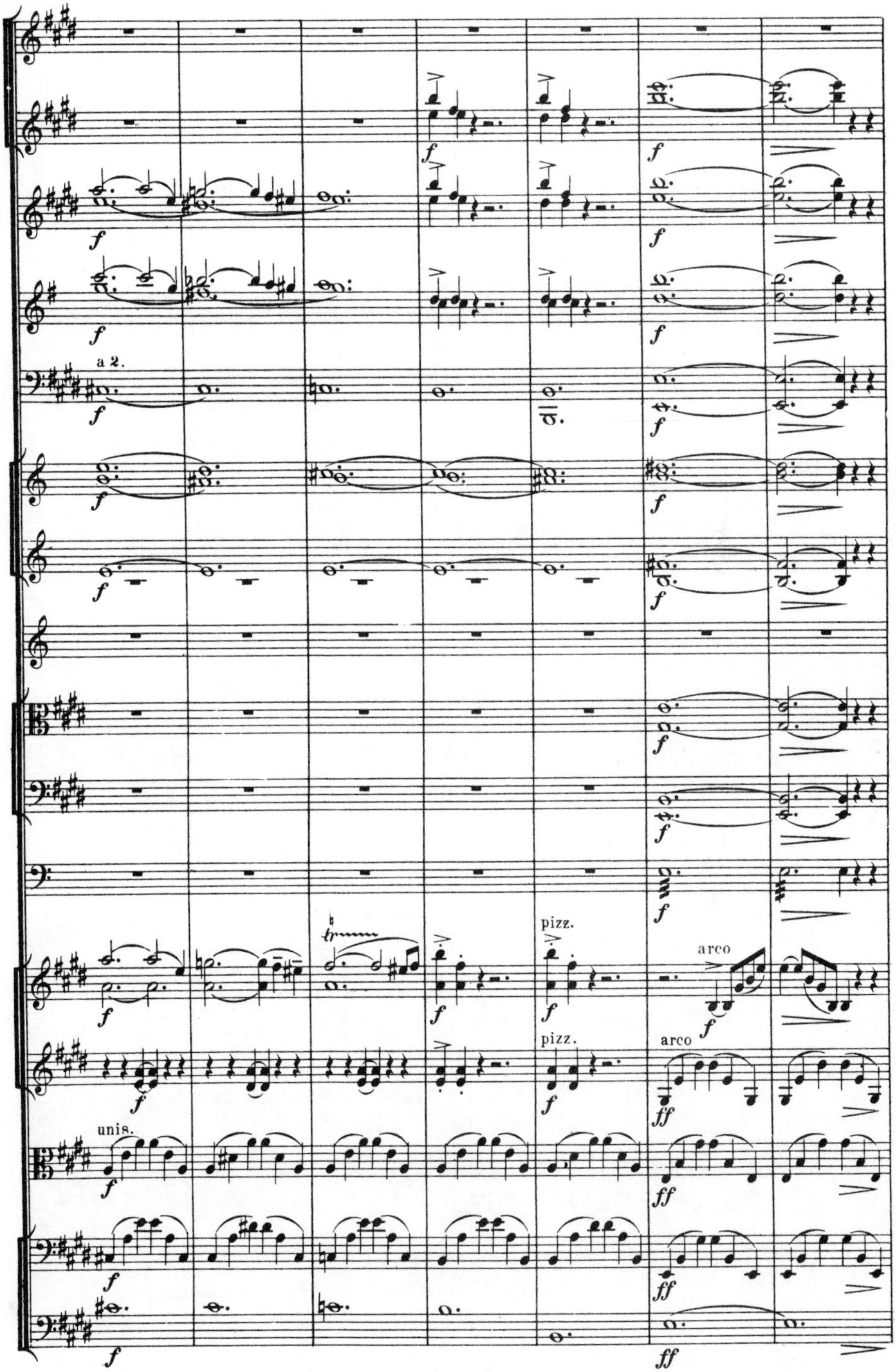

46

60

B Tranquillo.

105

119

125

133

141

144

181

187

190

193

222

231

II.

42 (II)

68

C

a tempo (un poco più animato)

a tempo (un poco più animato)

C

75

150

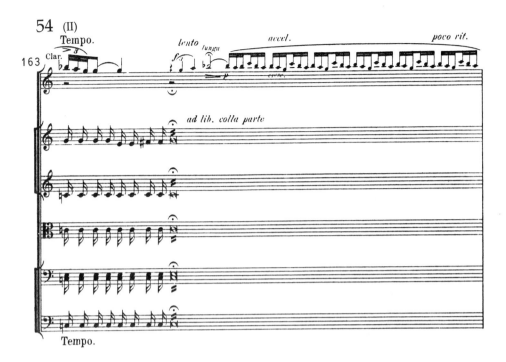

Vivace scherzando. ♩.= 132.

171

Violini I. divisi

Viol. II.

Viola.

V.C.

C.B.

Vivace scherzando. ♩.= 132.

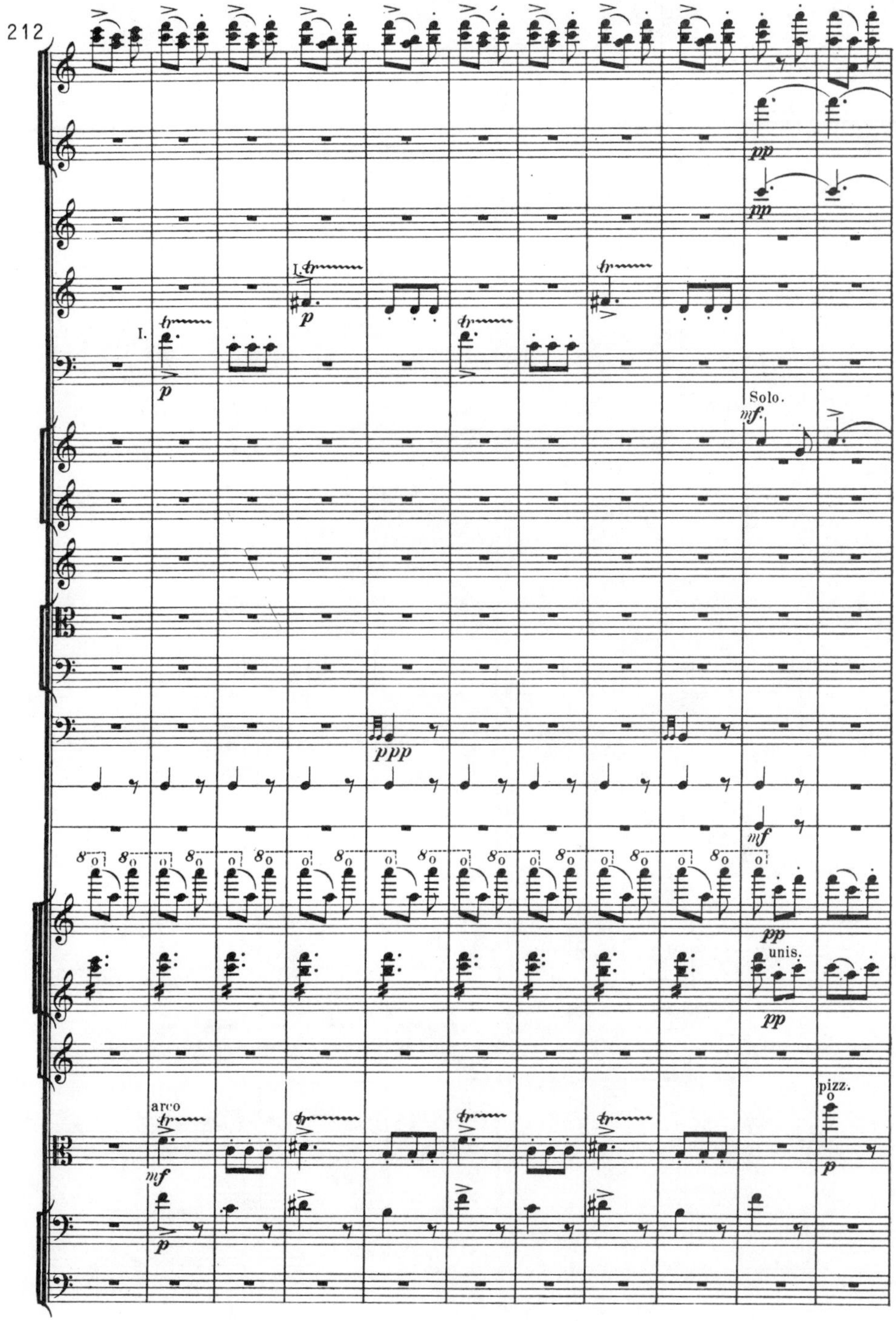
212
I.
p
I.
p
ppp
mf
Solo.
mf
pp
pp
pp
unis.
pp
arco
mf
pizz.
p
p

Poco stringendo

Poco stringendo

233

240

Tempo I. ♩ = 144.

1 Fl.picc.

2 Fl.gr.

Triang.

Piatti

Tempo I. ♩ = 144.

248

256

273

281

289

314

Moderato assai. ♩=♩=72.

322

328
M Allegro molto ed animato. ♩ = 152.
Fl. picc.
Fl.
I. Solo.
p
Ob.
I. Solo.
p
Clar.
I. Solo.
Fag.
Corni.
sf
sf
Trombe.
Tromb.
Tuba.
sf
sf
Timp.
sf
trem.
arco
pp
trem.
arco
pp
trem.
arco
pp
trem.
pp
arco
pizz.
p
M Allegro molto ed animato. ♩ = 152.

337

352

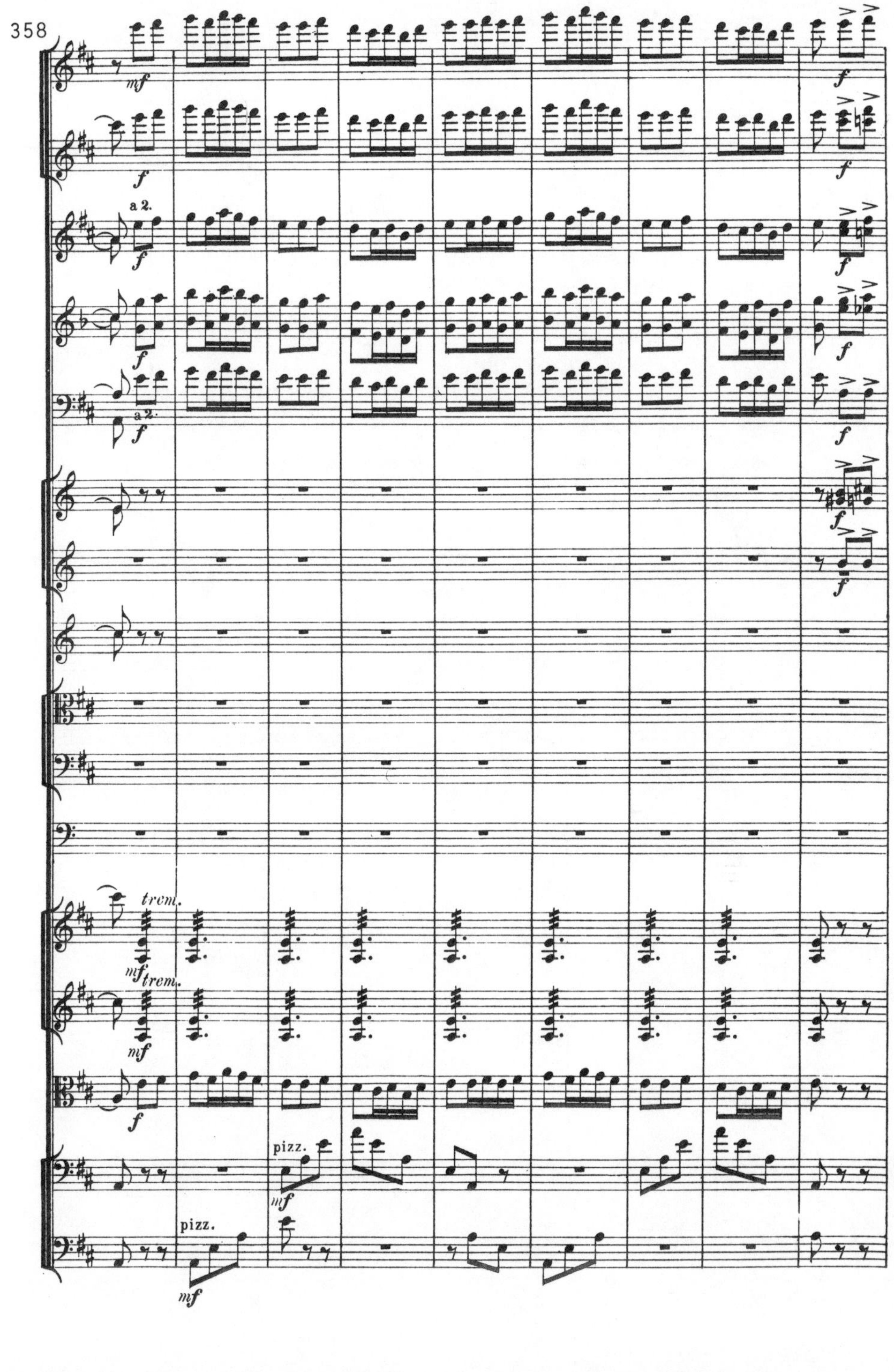
358
mf
f
a 2.
f
f
a 2.
f
f
f
f
f
f
f
trem.
mf
trem.
mf
f
pizz.
mf
pizz.
mf

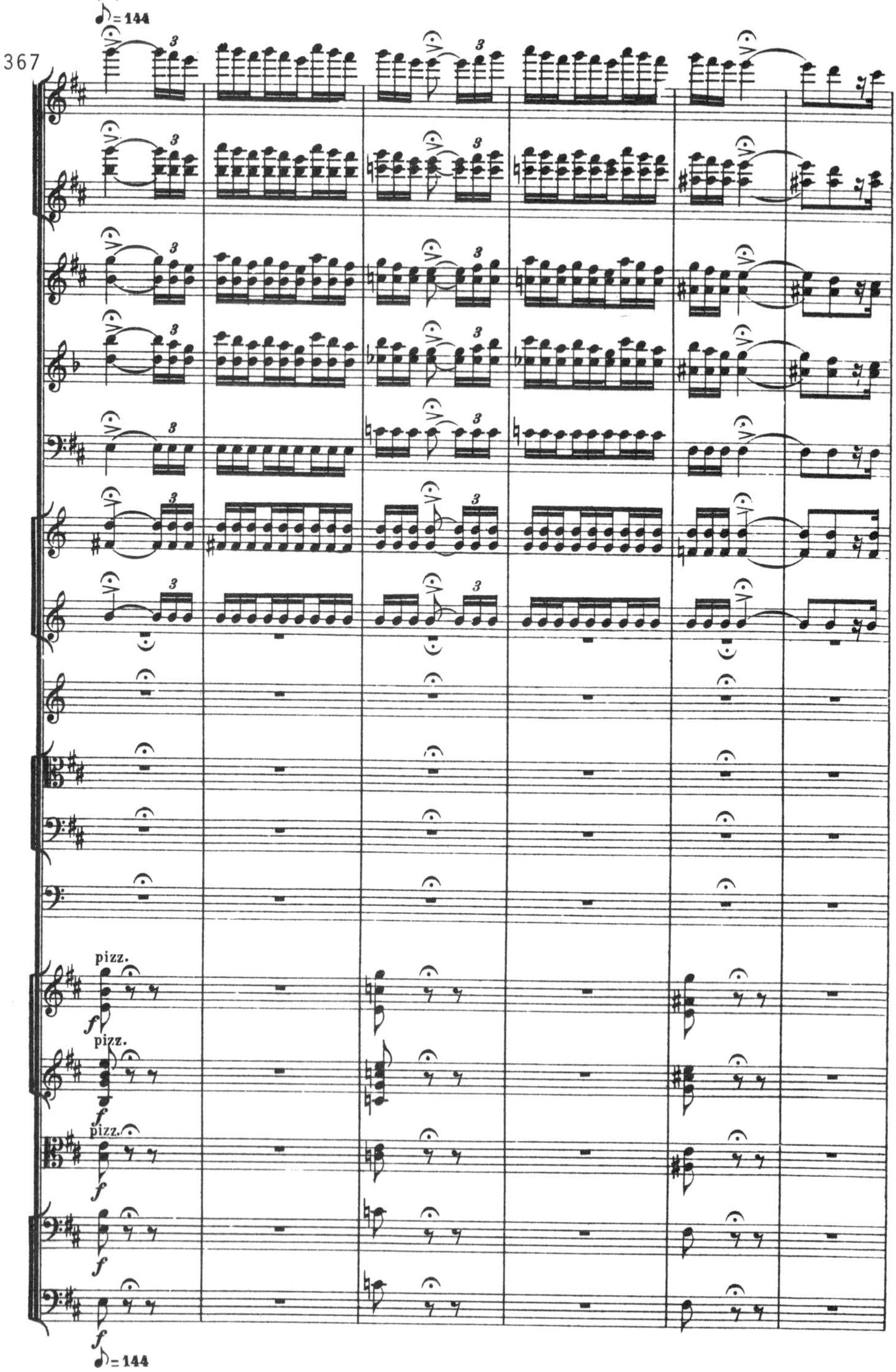
♪ = 144
367
pizz.
f
pizz.
f
pizz.
f
f
f
♪ = 144

381

389

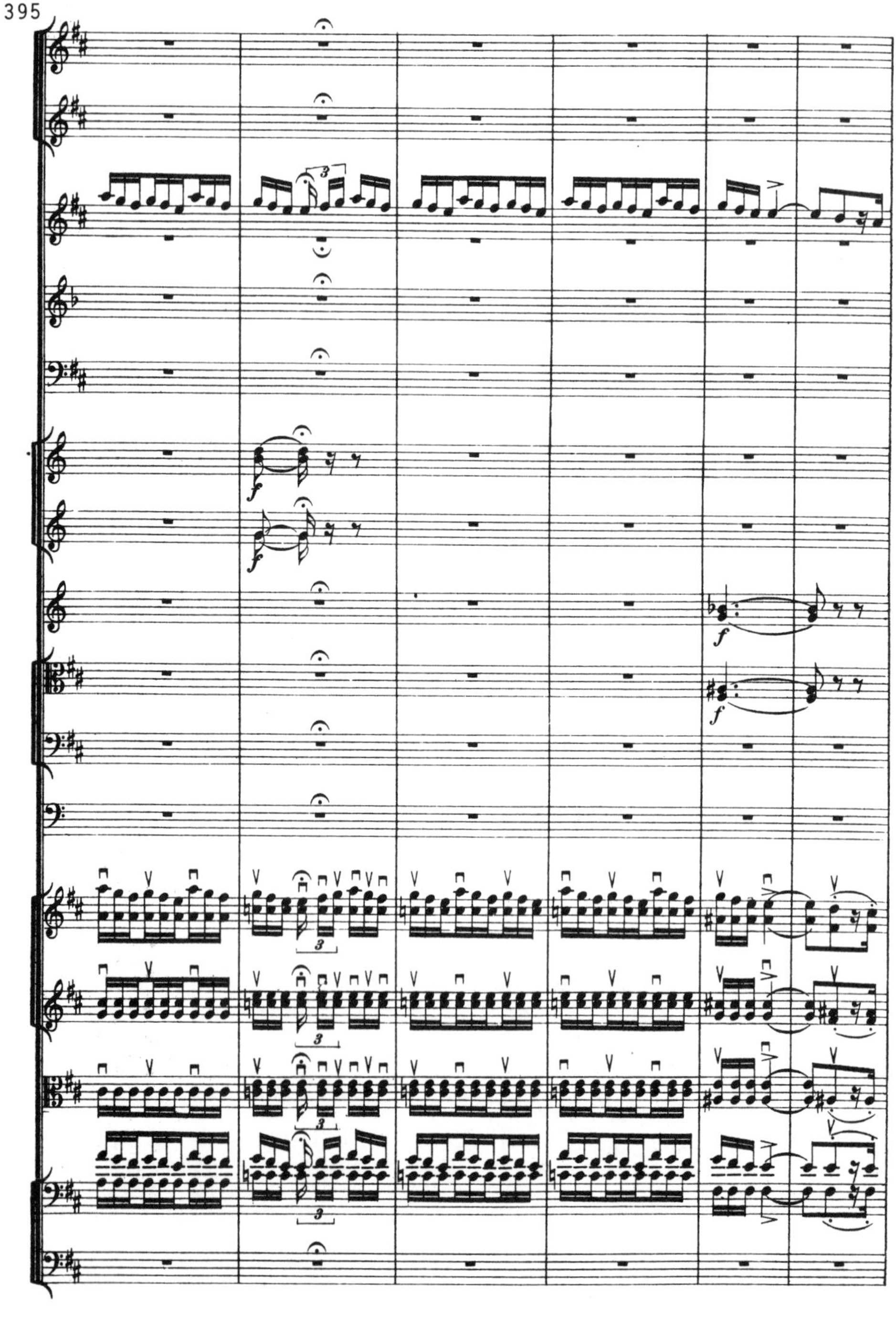
395
f
f
f
f

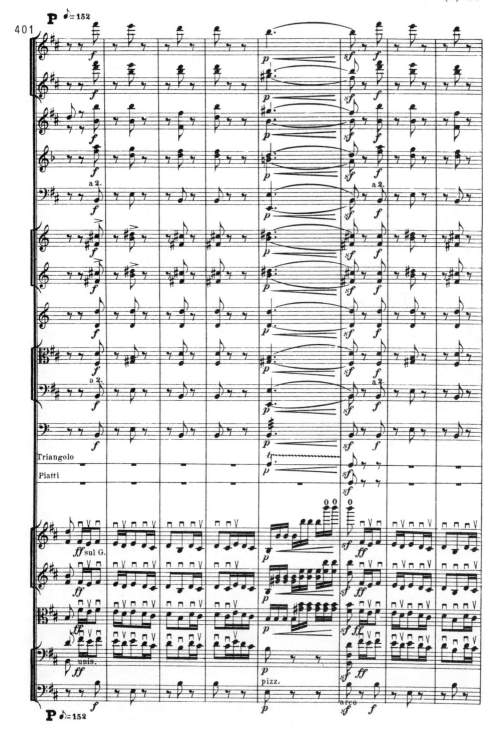

459

Animato. ♪=144

464

Animato. ♪=144

469

III.

95

58

66

88

95

99

103

123

I Come prima.

I Come prima.

171

180

205

IV.

133

Allegro molto e frenetico.

Allegro molto e frenetico.

75
a 2.
a 2.
a 2.
Tamburino.
Piatti.
arco
pizz.
arco
pizz.
arco
arco
pizz.
pizz.

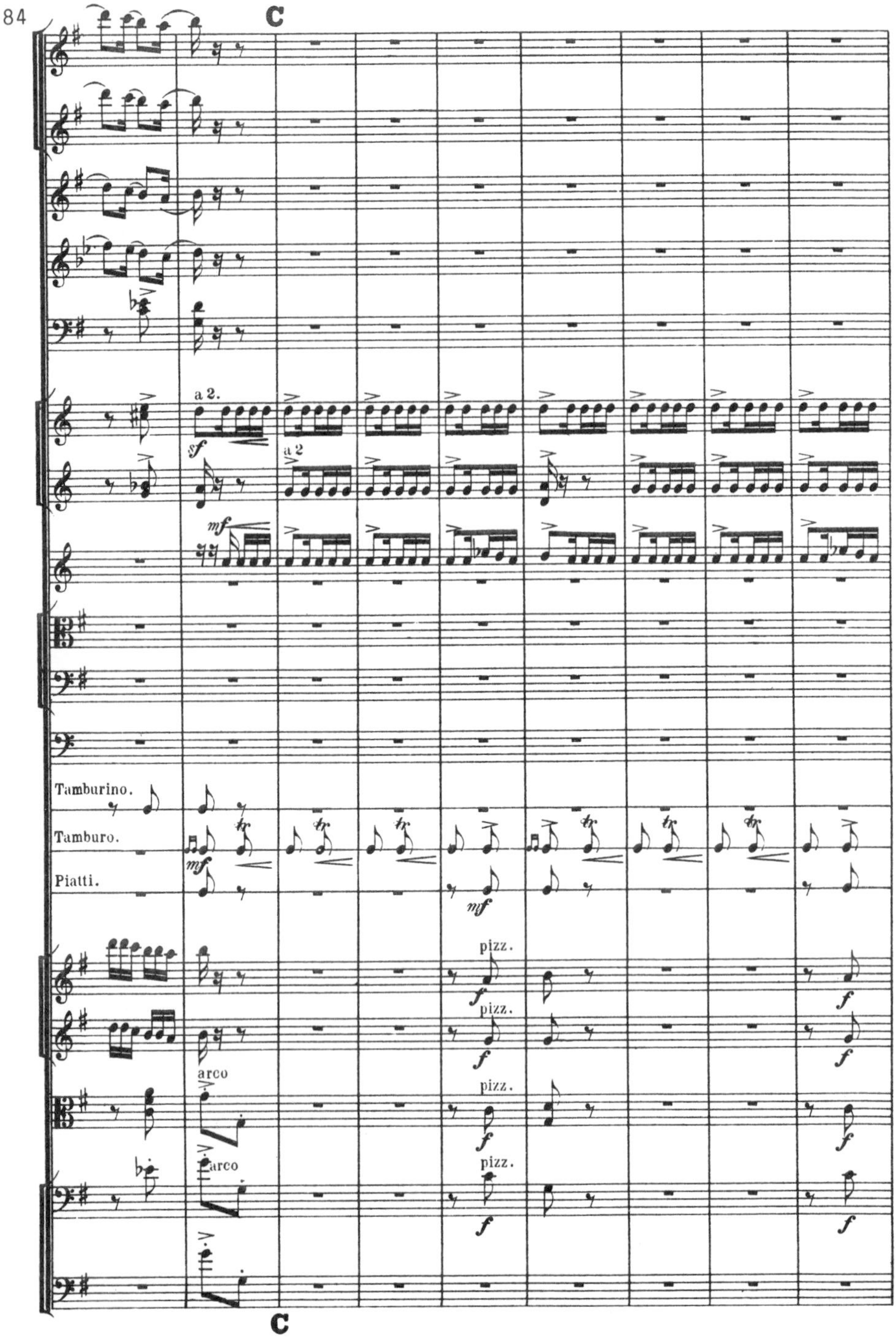
84
C
a 2.
sf
a 2
mf
Tamburino.
Tamburo.
tr
Piatti.
mf
pizz.
f
arco
C

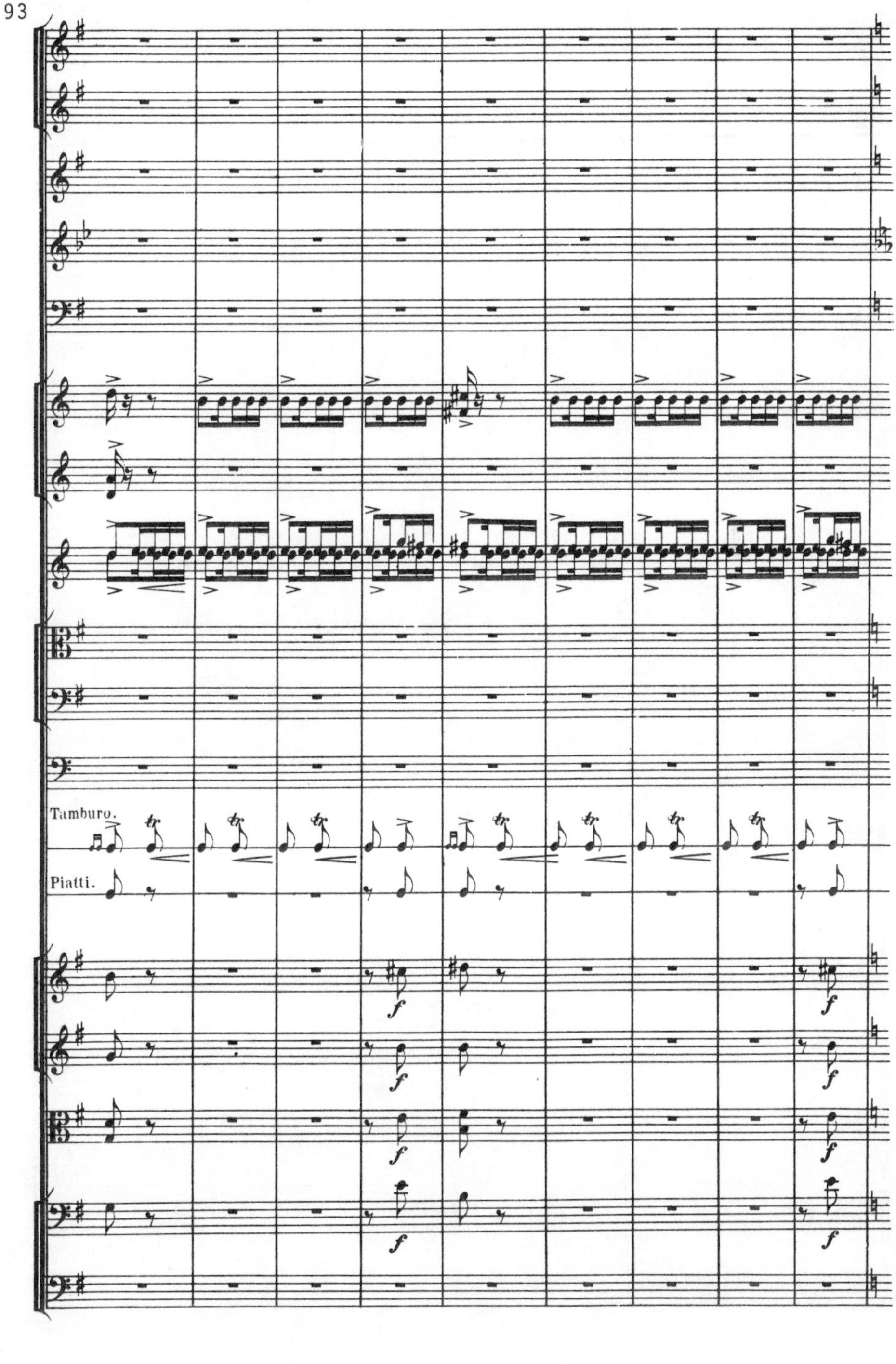
93
Tamburo.
Piatti.
tr
f

146 (IV)

127

166

197

251

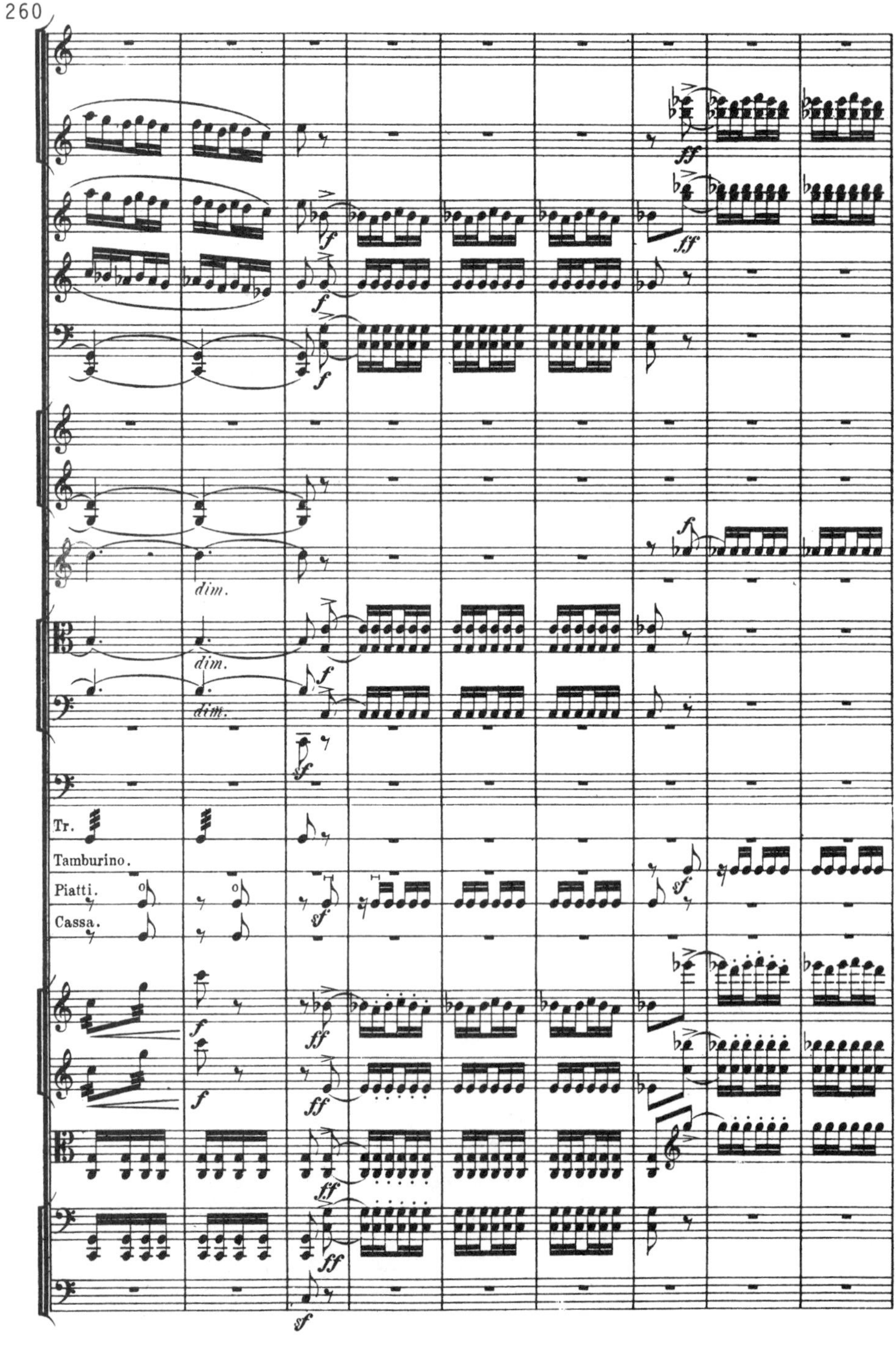
260
dim.
dim.
dim.
Tr.
Tamburino.
Piatti.
Cassa.
ff
f
sf

277

285

293

Triang.

Tamburino.

Tamburo.

Piatti.

Cassa.

375

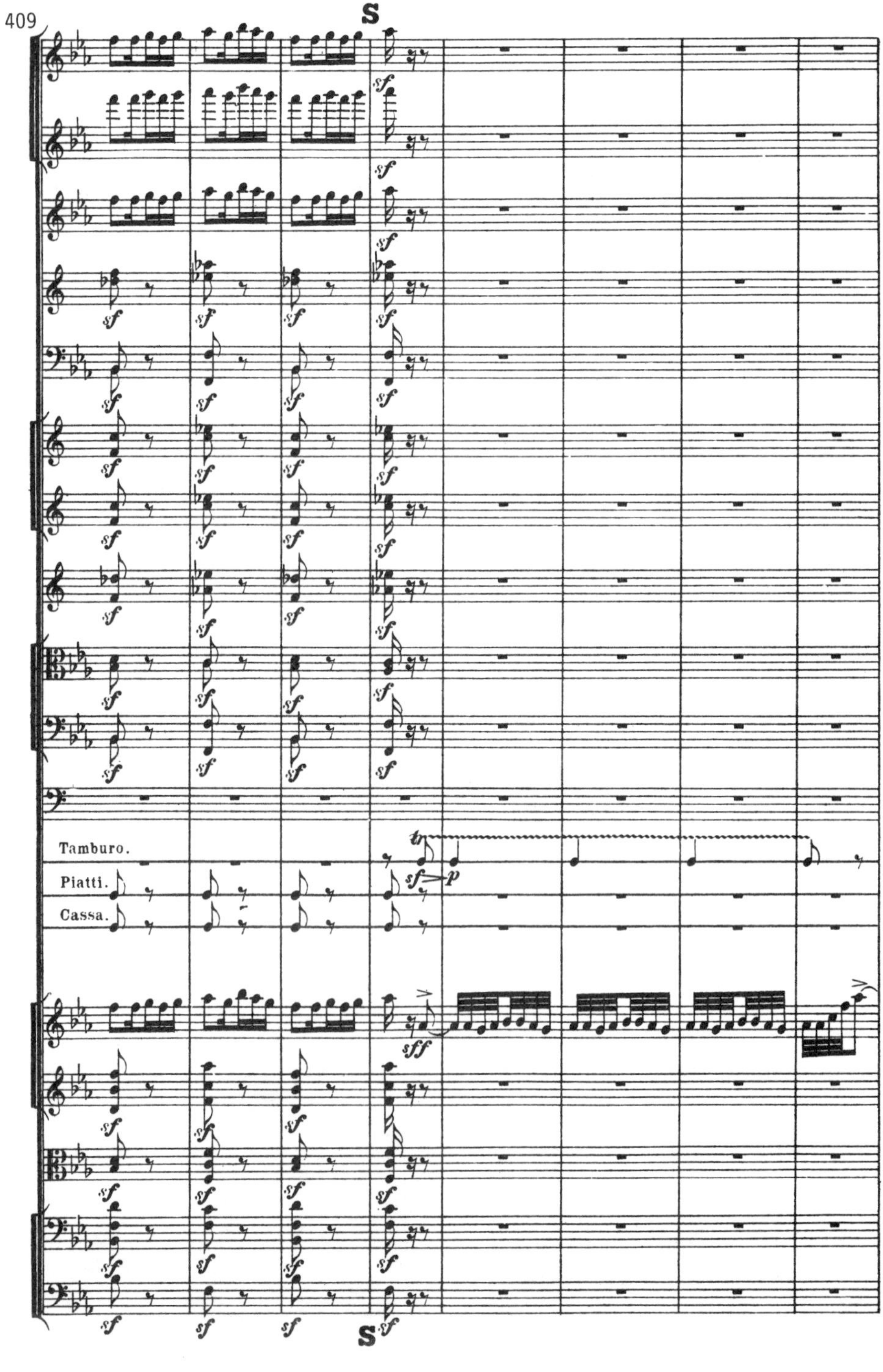
409
S
Tamburo.
Piatti.
Cassa.
S

462

480

500

192 (IV)

518

Tamburo

527

544

553

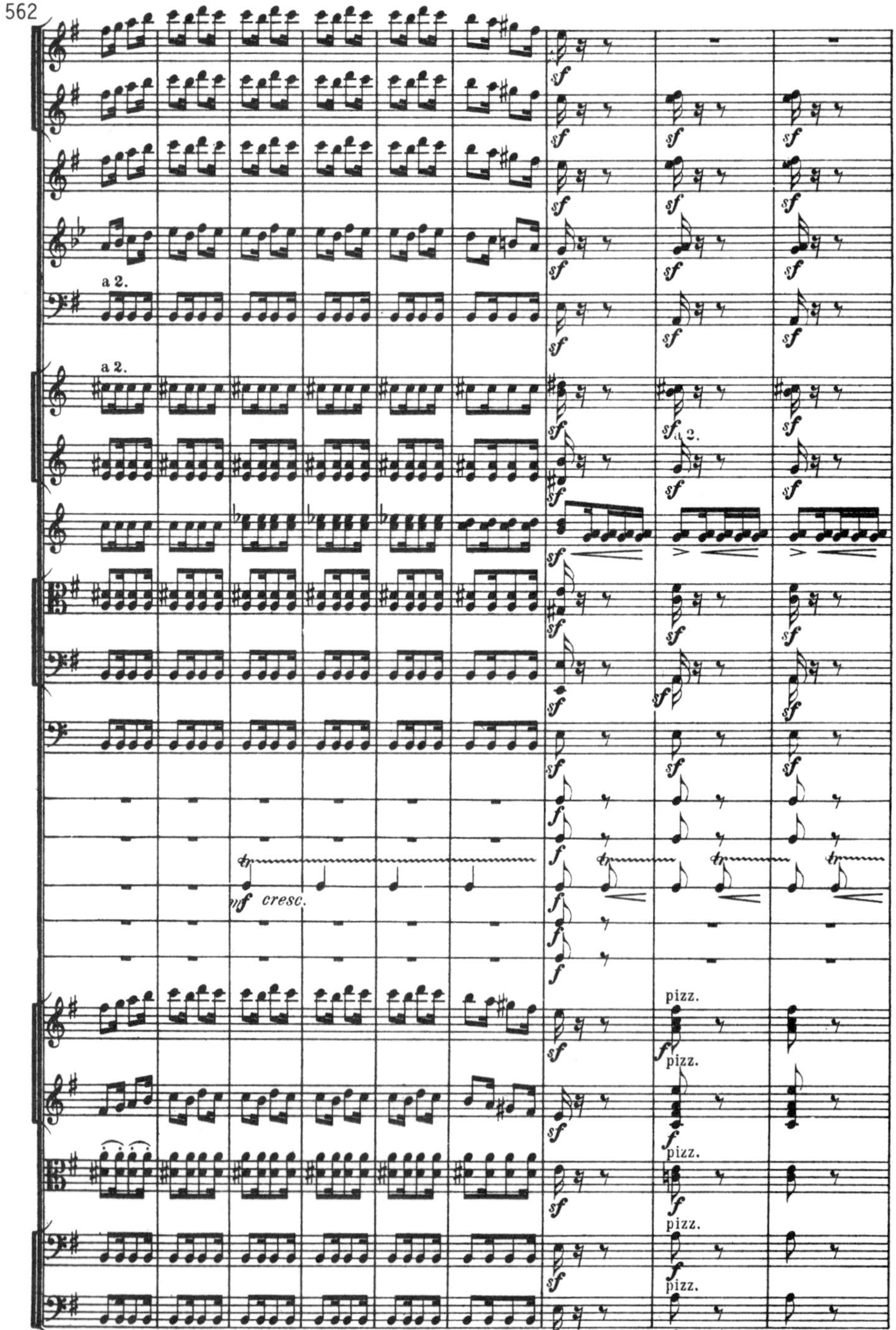
562
a 2.
a 2.
a 2.
mf cresc.
pizz.
pizz.
pizz.
pizz.
pizz.

584

Allegro non troppo e maestoso. ♩. = 60.

Allegro non troppo e maestoso. ♩. = 60.

204 (IV)

602

610

612

614

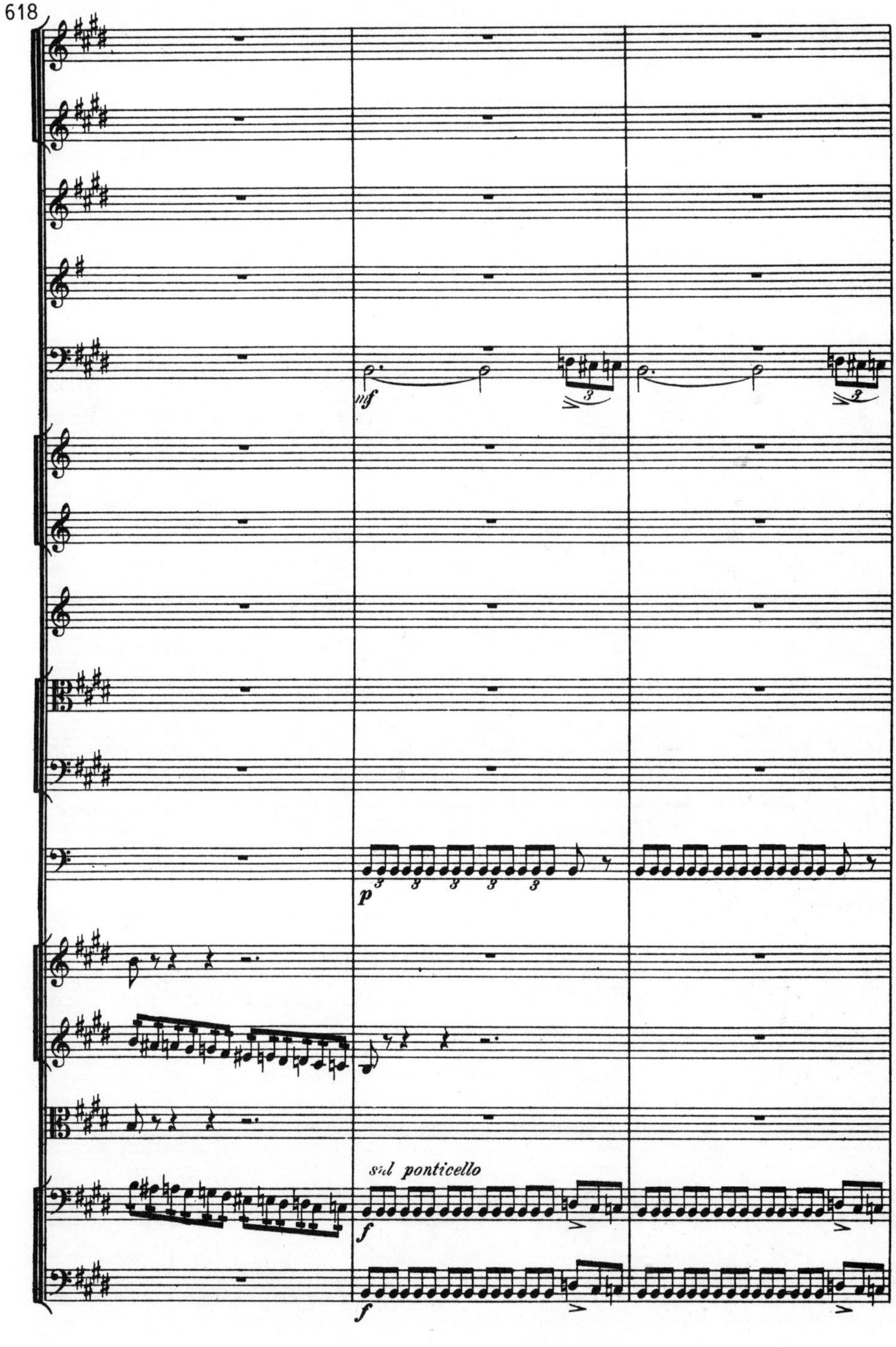
618
mf
p
sul ponticello
f
f

Poco più tranquillo. ♩. = 56.

Poco più tranquillo. ♩. = 56.

END OF EDITION

DOVER FULL-SIZE
ORCHESTRAL SCORES

THE SIX BRANDENBURG CONCERTOS AND THE FOUR ORCHESTRAL SUITES IN FULL SCORE, Johann Sebastian Bach. Complete standard Bach-Gesellschaft editions in large, clear format. Study score. 273pp. 9 x 12.   23376-6 Pa. **$12.95**

COMPLETE CONCERTI FOR SOLO KEYBOARD AND ORCHESTRA IN FULL SCORE, Johann Sebastian Bach. Bach's seven complete concerti for solo keyboard and orchestra in full score from the authoritative Bach-Gesellschaft edition. 206pp. 9 x 12.
24929-8 Pa. **$11.95**

THE THREE VIOLIN CONCERTI IN FULL SCORE, Johann Sebastian Bach. Concerto in A Minor, BWV 1041; Concerto in E Major, BWV 1042; and Concerto for Two Violins in D Minor, BWV 1043. Bach-Gesellschaft edition. 64pp. 9⅜ x 12¼.
25124-1 Pa. **$6.95**

GREAT ORGAN CONCERTI, OPP. 4 & 7, IN FULL SCORE, George Frideric Handel. 12 organ concerti composed by great Baroque master are reproduced in full score from the *Deutsche Handelgesellschaft* edition. 138pp. 9⅜ x 12¼.   24462-8 Pa. **$12.95**

COMPLETE CONCERTI GROSSI IN FULL SCORE, George Frideric Handel. Monumental Opus 6 Concerti Grossi, Opus 3 and "Alexander's Feast" Concerti Grossi—19 in all—reproduced from most authoritative edition. 258pp. 9⅜ x 12¼.   24187-4 Pa. **$13.95**

LATER SYMPHONIES, Wolfgang A. Mozart. Full orchestral scores to last symphonies (Nos. 35–41) reproduced from definitive Breitkopf & Härtel Complete Works edition. Study score. 285pp. 9 x 12.
23052-X Pa. **$12.95**

PIANO CONCERTOS NOS. 17–22, Wolfgang Amadeus Mozart. Six complete piano concertos in full score, with Mozart's own cadenzas for Nos. 17–19. Breitkopf & Härtel edition. Study score. 370pp. 9⅜ x 12¼.   23599-8 Pa. **$16.95**

PIANO CONCERTOS NOS. 23–27, Wolfgang Amadeus Mozart. Mozart's last five piano concertos in full score, plus cadenzas for Nos. 23 and 27, and the Concert Rondo in D Major, K.382. Breitkopf & Härtel edition. Study score. 310pp. 9⅜ x 12¼.
23600-5 Pa. **$16.95**

COMPLETE CONCERTI GROSSI IN FULL SCORE, Arcangelo Corelli. All 12 concerti in the famous late nineteenth-century edition prepared by violinist Joseph Joachim and musicologist Friedrich Chrysander. 240pp. 8⅜ x 11¼. 25606-5 Pa. **$12.95**

PIANO CONCERTOS NOS. 11–16 IN FULL SCORE, Wolfgang Amadeus Mozart. Authoritative Breitkopf & Härtel edition of six staples of the concerto repertoire, including Mozart's cadenzas for Nos. 12–16. 256pp. 9⅜ x 12¼. 25468-2 Pa. **$12.95**

NUTCRACKER SUITE IN FULL SCORE, Peter Ilyitch Tchaikovsky. Among the most popular ballet pieces ever created–a complete, inexpensive, high-quality score to study and enjoy. 128pp. 9 x 12. 25379-1 Pa. **$9.95**

TONE POEMS, SERIES I: DON JUAN, TOD UND VERKLARUNG, and DON QUIXOTE, Richard Strauss. Three of the most often performed and recorded works in entire orchestral repertoire, reproduced in full score from original editions. Study score. 286pp. 9⅜ x 12¼. (Available in U.S. only) 23754-0 Pa. **$14.95**

TONE POEMS, SERIES II: TILL EULENSPIEGELS LUSTIGE STREICHE, ALSO SPRACH ZARATHUSTRA, and EIN HELDENLEBEN, Richard Strauss. Three important orchestral works, including very popular *Till Eulenspiegel's Merry Pranks,* reproduced in full score from original editions. Study score. 315pp. 9⅜ x 12¼. (Available in U.S. only) 23755-9 Pa. **$14.95**

DAS LIED VON DER ERDE IN FULL SCORE, Gustav Mahler. Mahler's masterpiece, a fusion of song and symphony, reprinted from the original 1912 Universal Edition. English translations of song texts. 160pp. 9 x 12. 25657-X Pa. **$9.95**

SYMPHONIES NOS. 1 AND 2 IN FULL SCORE, Gustav Mahler. Unabridged, authoritative Austrian editions of Symphony No. 1 in D Major ("Titan") and Symphony No. 2 in C Minor ("Resurrection"). 384pp. 8⅛ x 11. 25473-9 Pa. **$16.95**

SYMPHONIES NOS. 3 AND 4 IN FULL SCORE, Gustav Mahler. Two brilliantly contrasting masterworks–one scored for a massive ensemble, the other for small orchestra and soloist–reprinted from authoritative Viennese editions. 368pp. 9⅜ x 12¼. 26166-2 Pa. **$18.95**

SYMPHONY NO. 8 IN FULL SCORE, Gustav Mahler. Superb authoritative edition of massive, complex "Symphony of a Thousand." Scored for orchestra, eight solo voices, double chorus, boys' choir and organ. Reprint of Izdatel'stvo "Muzyka," Moscow, edition. Translation of texts. 272pp. 9⅜ x 12¼. 26022-4 Pa. **$12.95**

DAPHNIS AND CHLOE IN FULL SCORE, Maurice Ravel. Definitive full-score edition of Ravel's rich musical settings of a Greek fable by Longus is reprinted here from the original French edition. 320pp. 9⅜ x 12¼. (Not available in France or Germany)
25826-2 Pa. **$15.95**

THREE GREAT ORCHESTRAL WORKS IN FULL SCORE, Claude Debussy. Three favorites by influential modernist: *Prélude à l'Après-midi d'un Faune, Nocturnes,* and *La Mer.* Reprinted from early French editions. 279pp. 9 x 12.
24441-5 Pa. **$13.95**

SYMPHONY IN D MINOR IN FULL SCORE, César Franck. Superb, authoritative edition of Franck's only symphony, an often-performed and recorded masterwork of late French romantic style. 160pp. 9 x 12.
25373-2 Pa. **$11.95**

THE GREAT WALTZES IN FULL SCORE, Johann Strauss, Jr. Complete scores of eight melodic masterpieces: The Beautiful Blue Danube, Emperor Waltz, Tales of the Vienna Woods, Wiener Blut, four more. Authoritative editions. 336pp. 8⅜ x 11¼.
26009-7 Pa. **$14.95**

THE FIREBIRD IN FULL SCORE (Original 1910 Version), Igor Stravinsky. Handsome, inexpensive edition of modern masterpiece, renowned for brilliant orchestration, glowing color. Authoritative Russian edition. 176pp. 9⅜ x 12¼. (Available in U.S. only)
25535-2 Pa. **$10.95**

PETRUSHKA IN FULL SCORE: Original Version, Igor Stravinsky. The definitive full-score edition of Stravinsky's masterful score for the great Ballets Russes 1911 production of *Petrushka.* 160pp. 9⅜ x 12¼. (Available in U.S. only)
25680-4 Pa. **$11.95**